Angel Promises

BASED ON LUKE 1:5-56

AS JEWS IN JERUSALEM GATHER IN THE TEMPLE FOR PRAYER, AN OLD PRIEST NAMED ZECHARIAH ENTERS THE HOLY PLACE TO MAKE AN OFFERING OF INCENSE.

THIS IS THE GREATEST DAY OF MY LIFE! AFTER ALL THESE YEARS, IT'S FINALLY MY TURN TO OFFER INCENSE ON GOD'S HOLY ALTAR.

BU... THE HOLY PLACE THAT THE PRIESTS BEGIN TO WONDER.

WHY IS ZECHARIAH PRAYING SO LONG?

I HOPE HE HASN'T DIED IN THERE. NO ONE ELSE IS ALLOWED IN THE HOLY PLACE.

MEANWHILE, THE FEARSOME ANGEL GABRIEL HAS APPEARED TO ZECHARIAH IN THE TEMPLE.

DO NOT BE AFRAID. YOU AND ELIZABETH WILL HAVE A SON. GOD WILL MAKE HIM MIGHTY AND FILLED WITH THE SPIRIT.

HIS NAME WILL BE JOHN, AND HE WILL PREPARE THE PEOPLE FOR GOD'S DELIVERER.

BUT WE'RE TOO OLD TO HAVE A BABY!

BECAUSE YOU DON'T BELIEVE, YOU WILL NOT BE ABLE TO TALK UNTIL THE BABY IS BORN.

1

AT LAST ZECHARIAH COMES OUT AND FACES THE PEOPLE. BUT HE CANNOT SPEAK! NO WORDS COME FROM HIS MOUTH.

WHAT HAPPENED IN THE HOLY PLACE OF GOD?

ZECHARIAH! WHAT'S WRONG? WHY DON'T YOU SPEAK TO ME?

ZECHARIAH CAN'T TELL ELIZABETH WHAT HAPPENED, SO HE WRITES DOWN EVERYTHING THE ANGEL TOLD HIM.

MARY CHERISHES THIS SECRET IN HER HEART, BUT SHE DOESN'T DARE TELL ANYONE ABOUT THE ANGEL'S PROMISE. JOSEPH IS A GOOD MAN, BUT IF PEOPLE FIND OUT SHE IS PREGNANT, SHE COULD BE KILLED.

I KNOW JOSEPH LOVES ME. BUT WOULD HE BELIEVE ME?

THE ANGEL HAD TOLD MARY THAT ELIZABETH WAS GOING TO HAVE A SON TOO. SO MARY GOES TO VISIT THE ONE PERSON SHE HOPES WILL UNDERSTAND. THE MOMENT ELIZABETH SEES MARY ...

MARY! YOU ARE BLESSED AMONG WOMEN! YOU ARE THE MOTHER OF OUR LORD!

MARY REALIZES THAT ELIZABETH KNOWS AND BELIEVES HER WONDERFUL SECRET. JOYFULLY SHE SINGS PRAISE TO GOD.

MY SOUL PRAISES THE LORD! AND MY SPIRIT REJOICES IN GOD, WHO SAVES ME! GOD IS MIGHTY, AND HE HAS DONE GREAT THINGS FOR ME. HIS NAME IS HOLY!

ZECHARIAH HAS BEEN SILENT FOR MONTHS. HE MOTIONS FOR A TABLET TO WRITE ON.

HIS NAME IS JOHN.

AT THAT VERY MOMENT, ZECHARIAH IS ABLE TO SPEAK AGAIN. HIS FIRST WORDS ARE A SONG OF WORSHIP TO THE LORD.

GIVE PRAISE TO THE LORD, THE GOD OF ISRAEL. HE HAS COME TO SET HIS PEOPLE FREE. HE HAS BEEN KIND TO HIS PEOPLE. AND YOU, MY CHILD, WILL BE CALLED A PROPHET OF THE MOST HIGH GOD.

BACK IN NAZARETH, JOSEPH HAS SECOND THOUGHTS ABOUT HIS ENGAGEMENT TO MARY BECAUSE HE DOESN'T KNOW ABOUT GOD'S PLAN FOR MARY AND HER BABY. SO ONE NIGHT, AN ANGEL COMES TO JOSEPH IN A DREAM.

DON'T BE AFRAID TO TAKE MARY AS YOUR WIFE. THE BABY INSIDE HER IS FROM THE HOLY SPIRIT. NAME HIM JESUS* BECAUSE HE WILL SAVE HIS PEOPLE FROM THEIR SINS.

* JESUS MEANS "GOD SAVES."

Birth of a Savior
BASED ON MATTHEW 1:18—2:11; LUKE 2:1-20

JOSEPH BELIEVES THE ANGEL AND MARRIES MARY, EVEN THOUGH HER PREGNANCY SEEMS SHAMEFUL TO OTHERS. ONE DAY THE NEWS COMES THAT THE ROMAN EMPEROR, CAESAR AUGUSTUS, WANTS TO HAVE A CENSUS. EVERYONE MUST GO TO HIS HOMETOWN TO BE COUNTED. EVEN THOUGH MARY'S BABY IS DUE ANY DAY NOW, JOSEPH AND MARY HAVE TO GO FROM NAZARETH TO BETHLEHEM.

WE'VE TRAVELED A LONG WAY. MY WIFE IS VERY TIRED. WE NEED A PLACE TO STAY.

I'M SORRY, BUT BETHLEHEM IS CROWDED BECAUSE OF THE CENSUS. WE DON'T HAVE ANY MORE EMPTY ROOMS.

EXHAUSTED, MARY AND JOSEPH HAVE NO CHOICE BUT TO STAY IN A STABLE. THERE, SURROUNDED BY ANIMALS, MARY GIVES BIRTH TO JESUS. SHE KEEPS HER BABY WARM IN A MANGER FILLED WITH HAY.

THAT SAME NIGHT, SOME SHEPHERDS ARE WATCHING THEIR SHEEP ON THE HILLS OUTSIDE BETHLEHEM. SUDDENLY, A GREAT LIGHT SPLITS THE NIGHT.

WHAT IS HAPPENING?

GOD SAVE US!

DON'T BE AFRAID. I BRING GOOD NEWS FOR YOU AND THE WHOLE WORLD.

TODAY IN THE CITY OF DAVID, A SAVIOR HAS BEEN BORN TO YOU. YOU WILL FIND THE BABY LYING IN A MANGER.

SUDDENLY THE SKY IS FILLED WITH A CHOIR OF ANGELS SINGING PRAISE TO GOD.

GLORY TO GOD IN THE HIGHEST, AND PEACE TO PEOPLE ON EARTH!

THE ANGELS LEAVE AND ONCE AGAIN DARKNESS FALLS UPON THE HILLS.

LET'S GO TO BETHLEHEM.

WE MUST SEE THE CHILD OF GOD FOR OURSELVES.

THE SHEPHERDS HURRY OFF TO BETHLEHEM.

Flight in the Night

BASED ON MATTHEW 2:12-18

THAT NIGHT, THE WISE MEN HAVE A STRANGE EXPERIENCE. GOD WARNS THEM NOT TO TRUST HEROD—AND NOT TO TELL HIM WHERE THE CHILD IS.

I HAD A DREAM—

SO DID I! GOD WARNED US NOT TO GO BACK TO JERUSALEM.

I HAD THE SAME DREAM. WE MUST GO HOME ANOTHER WAY.

THAT VERY NIGHT, HEROD'S SOLDIERS DESCEND ON BETHLEHEM AND BRUTALLY CARRY OUT THEIR EVIL ERRAND.

AND SO JEREMIAH'S PROPHECY IS FULFILLED: "THERE IS WEEPING AND GREAT MOURNING IN RAMAH. RACHEL WEEPS FOR HER CHILDREN AND WILL NOT BE COMFORTED, FOR THEY ARE NO MORE."

BUT JOSEPH AND MARY ARE ALREADY SAFELY ON THEIR WAY TO EGYPT, WHERE THEY'LL SPEND THE NEXT SEVERAL YEARS RAISING THEIR NEW BABY, THE SAVIOR OF THE WHOLE WORLD.